Through the Lens

Glimpses around old

Loch Ryan

by Jack Hunter

Dumfries and Galloway
Libraries, Information and Archives

First published 2005

Designed by Dumfries and Galloway Libraries, Information
and Archives. Set and printed by Solway Offset Services,
Catherinefield Industrial Estate, Dumfries for the publisher.

Dumfries and Galloway Libraries, Information and Archives
Central Support Unit, Catherine Street
Dumfries DG1 1JB
Tel: 01387 252070   Fax: 01387 260294
www.dumgal.gov.uk/lia

CULTURAL
SERVICES

ISBN 0 946280 68 1
Loch Ryan is number 28 in the
Dumfries and Galloway: Through the Lens series.
For a full list of our publications contact us at the above address.

ACKNOWLEDGEMENTS

I have to thank Mr J Compton, Mrs A Hannah,
Mr D Nelson, and Mr K Pearson for so
willingly providing or giving permission to use
photographs. For sharing their local knowledge
many local people have put me in their debt
particularly Mr J Alexander, Leswalt, Mr
J Compton, Kirkcolm, Mrs M Donaldson,
Stranraer, Mrs Hannah, Cairnryan, Mr W
MacCaig, Stranraer, Mrs McKie, Cairnryan,
Mr P Simpson, Kirkcolm, and Mrs E Wallace,
Cairnryan. Information has been obtained from
various books about the area and I am happy
to acknowledge my indebtedness to them.
Nevertheless, responsibility for all factual
errors, opinions, and generalisations rests with
me.

J Hunter

INTRODUCTION

The sea has always exerted a major influence on the area round Loch Ryan. The plethora of wrecks that litter the coast are evidence of its savage side. But the sea has also bestowed great benefits. As late as the 1940s it provided an essential transport link between the rural Rhinns and the outside world. And it was a valuable resource, yielding not only the more usual species of fish, particularly herring, but lordly types such as salmon and the famous Loch Ryan oysters. It also influences the climate, whose consequent mild winters suit dairy farming: the first Ayrshire herd in Galloway was at Mr James Ralston's Fineview farm just north of Kirkcolm around 1800. Early potatoes appreciated the same conditions, flourishing on the land facing the loch.

Of the three villages, Leswalt has a good claim to be the oldest. A church existed there in the mid-fourteenth century but the name may hint at even greater antiquity. While its origin is unclear, an authoritative source suggests it may come from the Welsh (British) language, which was spoken here before Gaelic, and mean "grass court or enclosure". If correct, this theory gives the village at least 1500 years of history. It is from Gaelic that Cairnryan takes its old name "Macherie" or "Machiryskeed" (the field of the hawthorn), employed until the mid-nineteenth century, when the Post Office declared it non-user-friendly. The landing place there must have been utilised by travellers from Ireland from a very early date.

Kirkcolm has also undergone a name change, originally being called Stewarton after the Stewarts of Garlies, who then owned Corsewall estate. The existing village dates from the 1780s but topographical evidence suggests that the old church in Corsewall House grounds stands on the site of a much earlier foundation. Does the dedication of the church to St Columba, which gives the village its modern name, reflect an old tradition of a connection with that saint, perhaps through the Cross Well near Corsewall lighthouse? And did some of the saint's followers land there, voluntarily or involuntarily, in transit between Ireland and Iona?

The area covered by this booklet was transformed and scarred by the multitudinous military installations of World War Two. The pictures are therefore a record of a largely vanished world.

1

INNERMESSAN MOTTE

Innermessan motte, with its shape like an inverted pudding bowl, is one of the most prominent features of the east side of Loch Ryan; in times past it was even more prominent before erosion took its toll: 160 years ago it was almost twice as high as it is today. And when it was built eight centuries ago it must have towered over the surrounding countryside. The motte is the earth base on which a twelfth century Anglo-Norman lord built his wooden castle. But the site at Innermessan had seen centuries of human activity before his imperious day. Finds from the valley of the adjacent burn prove the presence of human beings at least on a seasonal basis 10,000 years ago. And Innermessan's glory days post-dated the motte for in the fourteenth and fifteenth centuries a thriving town stood here, the largest in the Rhinns.

CLADDYHOUSE

Perched halfway up the hillside at the south end of Cairnryan, Claddyhouse contradictorily belies its name "the house on the beach". Perhaps that name, and the fact that the adjacent burn is called after the house, indicate an earlier building closer to the shore. Claddyhouse has for long been in the possession of the Dalrymple Hamiltons. Originally a summer house, with the main residence at Bargany near Girvan, "the house on the beach" eventually became the family home. The laird during the Second World War, Admiral Sir Frederick Dalrymple Hamilton, had a distinguished career on active service, which included command of five Russian convoys. However his most famous role was as captain of *HMS Rodney* in the action which sank the German battleship *Bismarck*. Coincidentally his son was serving as a midshipman in the other British battleship involved, *King George V*.

CAIRNRYAN PANORAMA

Cairn Point provides shelter from north and north-west winds to afford the landing place to which the village owes its existence. Its maritime connection is emphasised by the building on the left of the road in the foreground, part of which was used as a store by fishermen. Like many of Cairnryan's buildings it disappeared when Military Port No. 2 was built here in 1941. The telegraph poles and estate wall indicate the line of the pre-war road, following the shore out to the lighthouse and then turning north still close to the beach. The old parish manse just to right of centre still stands but not so the boathouse opposite it. The latter's position and substantial nature suggest it may have been used by Lochryan House. Behind the photographer, a croft stood till 1941 on the north part of the present ferry terminal complex.

4

CAIRNRYAN SCHOOL

The story of school provision at Cairnryan is a tangled tale. The first schoolmaster was probably Robert Lupton sometime in the 1840s. He also acted as precentor in the parish church at an annual salary of £3. This building was almost certainly put up when the act of 1872 introduced state, free, compulsory education. It stood on the seaward side of the road close to the present entrance to the P & O terminal. It was demolished in 1941 to make way for the military harbour and the Army built a wooden hut as replacement on the site of the present football field. When post-war munitions dumping started from the port, the school was prudently moved into the former YMCA building, now the Rhins of Galloway facility. However at the age of around eight, pupils had to move to Stranraer; eventually all pupils were transferred there.

CAIRNRYAN, SOUTH END

At its south end, the pre-war village started just beyond the filling station: the little dividing wall on the right is still there. The shop with the sign beside the door was converted from a private house by Jimmy Keenan. The large building with two dormer windows and signs above the door is another shop, the grocer's and post office run by the legendary Mrs Aitken. During World War Two Mrs Aitken took boarders, servicemen's wives and later engineers supervising construction of Mulberry harbour components. With the former, part of the cost was paid in kind, the ladies having to assist with household tasks. The car at the door may be her well known vehicle, which was garaged in the part of the building on the seaward side not used as a fishermen's store. The building immediately beyond Mrs Aitken's was the Cross Keys Inn.

THE CROSS KEYS INN

Members of Lochryan Yacht Club relax outside the Cross Keys, today the "Auld Cairn", on their June outing in 1892. The inn was also popular for informal Sunday outings by boat from Stranraer since the participants became bona fide travellers and so sidestepped the strict Scottish laws against Sabbath drinking. Archibald McCutcheon's predecessor as licensee in 1824 was John Gordon but the inn name indicates a much longer history. Inns with religious names like this often date from medieval times, when they were used, by pilgrims. In this case the likelihood exists that travellers from Ireland bound for the shrine of St Ninian at Whithorn, Scotland's premier pilgrim destination, landed here and then continued their journey by foot. The attire of the group pictured suggests that the weather for their outing was less than ideal.

7

CAIRNRYAN FROM THE NORTH SHORE

The coastguard station with its signal mast is right of centre in the middleground. To the left of the mast the last house in the row was at this time the police station and at a later date became the post office. The fact that its neighbour is a cottage dates the picture as pre-1899 for in that year the parish church hall was built beside the police station. Behind the main street, just left of centre, the Free Church looms large. After the (United) Free Church rejoined the Church of Scotland in 1929 the building was surplus to ecclesiastical requirements. It was then bought by the Thomson family and used for dances, film shows, and badminton, being known as Thomsons' Hall. Following wartime occupation by the Army it reverted to those functions and was eventually taken over by the community until replaced by the present community hall.

CAIRNRYAN, NORTH END

The later date of this view is proved by the loss of bell tower from the Free Church, perhaps signifying its post-1929 secularisation, and appearance of the parish church hall beside the police station. On the other side of the road the coastguard station has grown, with the addition of a watch-tower, into a substantial two-storey building. It eventually closed down and became a private dwelling known as "The Boathouse", occupied for many years by Miss Macgregor, who taught the piano. The tall stone angling out from between the second and third houses on the left is the former Jougs Stone, to which offenders were attached by an iron collar for public humiliation and perhaps pelted with missiles for their sins. However it very probably is of much older date and may well be a 5,000 year-old standing stone similar to two others in the area.

CAIRNRYAN MAIN STREET

This southward-looking view is dominated by the premises where Mrs McFadzean, as the sign above the door testifies, dispensed teas and refreshments. Now known as *Lochview* it also provided accommodation, a reminder that before World War Two Cairnryan was a holiday resort popular with those seeking quietness and good seabathing. In stormy weather it was also popular with travellers of a different kind for the Cairn Pool directly opposite the village, with its seven fathoms of water, provided shelter for even the largest vessels. This fact was commented on as far back as 1791, when it was pointed out that many vessels from the West Indies bound for the Clyde took refuge here in adverse weather. At one time Cairnryan enjoyed good steamer connections with both the Glasgow-Stranraer and Belfast – Stranraer services calling. *Lochview* is situated just south of the gap in the centre of the village.

FUND-RAISING ENTERTAINMENT
The cast of an entertainment performed in Thomsons' Hall in May, 1935, in aid of the Garrick Cottage Hospital Extension Fund. It took the form of 22 scenes from *The Sleeping Beauty* presented as tableaux vivants, that is without movement or speech. The latter was provided by Miss Jamieson as reader. Two performances were staged, one on Wednesday evening and the second on Saturday afternoon; both were well attended. At the close of the second performance Mrs Aitken presented each participant with a gift of sweets, doubtless much appreciated, which collectively must have greatly depleted the stocks of her confectionery department. Reasonably easy to identify among the cast are King R. Woodley, Queen C. Dalrymple Hamilton (Miss Christian?), Bad Fairy M. Turriff, and Old Man S. Neville. Both Cook and Cook's Boy, with suitable headgear, were members of the Thomson family, as were four other participants.

LIGHTHOUSE

Cairnryan lighthouse, now shorn of its keepers' cottages, was built on Cairn Point in 1847 by Alan Stevenson of the famous lighthouse-building family. A claim 30 years later that it was originally intended merely as a landmark seems unlikely but is difficult to ignore. Almost 150 years earlier, in 1702, a very different structure had been proposed for Cairn Point, then known as Whiteforeland, by Major Andrew Agnew of Lochryan estate. On the resumption of war with France he petitioned the Scottish Privy Council to construct a fort there with six cannon to prevent a repetition of the constant raids on Loch Ryan by French privateers, which had cost the Major and his terrified tenants dear. During the last bout of hostilities French raiding parties had ravaged the estate lands, carrying away not only cattle but joists and flooring from houses. His appeal was unsuccessful.

ENTRANCE TO LOCHRYAN HOUSE

The area just north of the village was transformed by the building of the military port. The bottom half of the picture shows a vanished landscape with only two features remaining: the graveyard behind the church with the Wallace mausoleum and the small tower to its right. The pre-war A77 snakes along the shore while the wall on the far right, largely disappeared, gives the approximate line of the modern road. Between the two, on this side of the church, is the deer park. When construction of the port began in 1941 the advance party of soldiers pitched their tents on the bowling green in the left foreground doubtless to local consternation. The road winding up Laird's Hill in the background is the old road north. The former entrance to Lochryan House with its four gate pillars and Scots baronial lodge is an imposing one.

13

LOCHRYAN HOUSE DEER PARK

Fallow deer safely graze in the deer park in front of Lochryan House. An early twentieth century traveller recorded that the herd was a large one. Just out of sight to the left is a small, round tower in the wall (clearly seen in the previous picture) known as The Pulpit. Before a church was built in Cairnryan in 1841 and with the parish church seven miles away, the Inch minister used to hold occasional services here, officiating from The Pulpit while the congregation sat on the grass. The turret still stands today at the north end of the white fence fronting the wartime dockyard but sadly is almost obscured by vegetation. Just out of sight on the hill in the top right-hand corner is a slate quarry, which was in operation as early as the second half of the eighteenth century.

LOCHRYAN HOUSE

In 1701 Andrew Agnew of Croach or Lochryan estate left the old house on the edge of the plateau above the Claddy Glen and moved to a new residence on the shore behind Cairn Point. A professional soldier, Agnew must have been impressed by the chateaux he had seen while campaigning in France and Flanders for he built Lochryan House in a similar style. The original main entrance to the considerably altered building may have been on the east side facing the hill. Agnew's descendants still own the house today; his heiress daughter married Sir Thomas Wallace of Craigie outside Ayr. His granddaughter, Mrs Dunlop, was a patron and valued friend of Robert Burns. A later owner, General Alexander Wallace, greatly distinguished himself in the Peninsular War. The eagle, the Agnew crest, surmounting each gatepillar is a reminder that Andrew Agnew was related to the Lochnaw family.

15

CAIRNRYAN CHURCH

Rather unkindly described in an old guidebook as "a building of no special interest", Cairnryan church was built in 1841 to save local people the long journey to the parish church near Castle Kennedy. At that time the surrounding area was given only limited parish status, not achieving full status as Lochryan parish until 1858. The new parish had a short life for in 1938 it was united with Glenapp across the county boundary in Ayrshire. In another change it was reunited with Inch parish in 1985 and the church eventually closed. The building was demolished in 1990 to create more room in the graveyard. No trace of the thatched cottage survives but the house beyond the church still stands. The road in the foreground is the old A77.

VISITING YACHT
Lord Inchcape's yacht *The Rover* lies elegantly off Cairnryan in the late 1920s. She was virtually in home waters for her owner was also proprietor of Glenapp castle and estate and in 1930 his acquisition of the neighbouring Finnarts estate gave him frontage on Loch Ryan. Sea transport was an entirely appropriate form of travel for Lord Inchcape, a giant of British shipping and chairman of the P. & O. line. *The Rover* was in the loch again in 1931 for a fairly spectacular rendezvous between Lord Inchcape and the recently retired chairman of Imperial Airways, who arrived appropriately by three-engined flying boat. Lord Inchcape had plans to build a harbour at Finnarts Bay, but they did not materialise. Other steam yachts and their wealthy owners, including the Cadbury family, visited Loch Ryan at this time.

NORTH FROM CAIRNRYAN

Just beyond *Marchburn,* the white house in the centre of the picture, the Galloway Burn marks the boundary between the former counties of Wigtownshire and Ayrshire. Which line the road north from Cairnryan followed is a much discussed question. That taken by the A77, seen on the right, is of no great antiquity. It probably dates from the military road of 1782, although the latter may have run higher up the hillside, having ascended part of the way up Laird's Hill. The older coach road ran to the top of that hill and along the edge of the plateau, in the right background, before descending into Glenapp. The possibility that the original road ran along the bottom of the cliffs, on the left, lacks supporting evidence. It would be inadvisable to imitate the example of the strolling couple today.

INCISED BOULDER, DALLY BAY

This puzzling, incised boulder lies on the rocky headland at the south end of Dally Bay. The style of carving suggests it is on no great antiquity. The solution to the puzzle may lie in an event at the close of the eighteenth century. At the seaward end of the headland a track makes use of a natural pass through the rock to link the landing place at the bay with the farms to the south. Around 1800 the local laird, Major Ross of Airies, had the cutting deepened and widened to improve the road. For labour he used men of the Sutherland Fencibles (militia) regiment who had been disbanded after the end of a rebellion in Ireland, probably that of the United Irishmen in 1798. Perhaps one of the militiamen used a meal break and one of the squad's drills to incise this graffito.

CORSEWALL LIGHTHOUSE

Situated on the north-west tip of the Rhinns peninsula, Corsewall lighthouse is the principal leading light into the Firth of Clyde for ships coming from the south. Designed by Robert Stevenson of the famous family of lighthouse builders and constructed of local whinstone, it came into operation in 1816. The original light apparatus was transferred to Corsewall from the famous Bell Rock lighthouse off the east coast of Scotland. An automated system has long since replaced the former staff of three keepers and their accommodation is now a hotel. The importance of Corsewall Point with its commanding situation was recognised long before the age of Robert Stevenson. Nearly two thousand years previously the Iron Age inhabitants of the area built a fort on Dunskirloch promontory just 200 metres east of the lighthouse. The only remaining trace of it is a spread of rubble from its defensive wall.

BARNEY MAGEE'S COTTAGE

Barney Magee's cottage stands on a small inlet half-a-mile east of Corsewall lighthouse. The gentleman seated on the boat may be Barney himself, who died in 1905. The cottage is part of the former mill building which gave the inlet its name, Portmullin. The aperture in the west wall for the drive shaft from the mill wheel is still visible although the stream that provided the water power is so small that a dam and reservoir must have been necessary and milling was surely on a limited scale. As the rowing boat shows, local people also used the inlet to fish for salmon and lobsters. During the building of Corsewall lighthouse the engineer in charge of the project lived here.

21

MAHAAR SCHOOL

Mahaar school football team with their headmaster Mr Charles Smith, later head of Sheuchan primary, provide a graphic illustration of the extent of rural depopulation in Wigtownshire in the last 50 years for the school, which had 75 pupils in 1954, has been closed for 40 years. Opened about 1819 in what is reckoned the oldest school building in the county, Mahaar was originally the only school in Kirkcolm parish and for long remained the parish school because of its central position. It originally consisted of a single room and the schoolmaster's salary in the early days was £17 per annum. Pupils paid fees of between one shilling and two shillings and sixpence a month. For most of the second half of the twentieth century the tenant of nearby Mahaar farm, Mr John F. Niven, was education convener of Wigtown County Council.

CORSEWALL MILL
Corsewall mill north of Kirkcolm dates from the late 18th century (it appears on a 1782 map) but has been added to several times. It was water-powered with an overshot millwheel, which was replaced by a turbine about 1900. Previously, around 1870, a steam engine had been installed to give additional power; its chimney stack can clearly be seen here. The kiln for drying the grain had a metal floor and to find out if the temperature was high enough the miller apparently spat on the floor and observed how long it took for the bubbles to expand. For most of its existence the mill's tenants were the famous Hannay family. When they eventually concentrated production on their Stranraer mill, Corsewall closed. Attempts to demolish it by dynamiting in the 1960s ceased after damage to neighbouring property and it was later destroyed by fire.

23

MILTON

The name suggests the house stands on the site of a former clachan connected with nearby Corsewall mill; traces of buildings behind it may show the site of this settlement. Built in 1859, *Milton* has had only two owners, the McDowall family and the Compton family. Its builder, John McDowall, had diversified business interests: a joinery business, coffin making, and possession of the salmon fishing rights at The Wig and Lady Bay. His business accounts for the mid-nineteenth century reveal a very different commercial world from today: his hourly rate was one shilling and ninepence (9p) and when his five workmen were given a day off for the local agricultural show, they lost a day's pay. Although today *Milton* stands by the roadside, the road formerly ran well behind it along the crest of a wooded ridge. The realignment was to bring the highway closer to the mill.

24

CORSEWALL HOUSE

Corsewall House outside Kirkcolm was built as a dower house before 1810, when the estate was owned by the Earls of Galloway. It was enlarged by Dr James Moore of Glasgow when he was gifted the house and part of the estate by Glasgow banker Robert Carrick. Carrick's gift was the result of his admiration for Moore's brother, General Sir John, the hero of the Battle of Corunna and subject of a statue in Glasgow's George Square. It was further enlarged when it passed to the (Carrick) Buchanans of Drumpellier although some of those extensions have been removed. This photograph was taken before 1905 as the angled rear wing on the east (right) side was added in that year. As the foreground shows, Corsewall House was famous for its gardens, especially the wealth of exotic shrubs which thrived in the sheltered, maritime location.

25

BOAT BANK

Although Kirkcolm was not primarily a fishing village, its proximity to the sea ensured it developed maritime links. Some fishing went on in Loch Ryan from rowing boats, which were kept at the Boat Bank (now almost lost to erosion). As well as catching herring, haddock, and cod, the fishermen gathered oysters on The Scar. However by 1950 fishing as an occupation had virtually disappeared. In 1837 the parish could also boast three small vessels employed in the coasting trade. But Kirkcolm's main claim to maritime fame was as a nursery for seafarers. This was largely due to the work of John Wright, *The Whaleback Dominie*, who died in 1884. A veteran of whale fishing in The South Seas, in his retirement he opened a school in the parish to teach the skills of seamanship, the fame of which attracted pupils from far beyond the local area.

KIRKCOLM, SOUTH END

The maritime theme continues in this view of the south end of Kirkcolm village: the two poles on the right were outsize *clothes poles* for drying fishing nets. The building in the left middleground with two gable windows belonged at one time to a fishing family called Garrett and the bend in the road at that point is locally known as Garretts' Corner. In the left foreground the Corsewall Arms hotel has a lamp above its main entrance while the large doorway beyond leads to the hotel stables. The first floor of the next building accommodated Brown's Hall. Since the public hall was not built until 1928, Brown's Hall presumably was the venue for the farmers', small farmers', ploughmen's, and sailors' balls, which collectively enlivened the nineteenth century Kirkcolm winter. In the early twenties films were shown here and latterly it was used for carpet bowling.

KIRKCOLM, MAIN STREET

Here, as we look north, the eye is caught by the dazzling stretch of pavement fronting the second house on the right while all else is cobbled. Unsurprisingly this was the residence of mason Willie Campbell, who possibly features in the picture. From his reluctance to accept large jobs he was locally known as "The Mousehole Mason". Two doors beyond is the former Commercial Hotel, latterly The Blue Peter, while next door to it the single storey house was the home of the council roadman. On the opposite side of the road the children are congregated hopefully outside Miss Shennan's grocery shop, one of three such establishments which the village formerly possessed. The buildings on the left are not on the original street line. This was further back and some of the houses still stand today, used as outhouses, behind those in the picture.

KIRKCOLM, NORTH END

The top end of Kirkcolm village has not changed radically since this 1895 picture. At that time the fourth house on the right was the post office and registrar's office, as shown by the wooden signboard on the wall. The house on the left with the vegetation-covered front, the home for 100 years of the McMeekan family, is known as *The Inkpot* or *Pepper Pot* because of its shape. The large building beyond was at one time a general store while Baillie's grocery shop was situated behind the photographer. A picture of Kirkcolm village in the 1920s, under the inelegant pseudonym of Kirkleswalt, is given in the autobiographical novel *Palace of Green Days* by the noted Scots short story writer Fred Urquhart. In the 1920s Urquhart's father was chauffeur to the owner of Corsewall estate.

KIRKCOLM SCHOOL GROUP

Teacher Mrs Heron poses with Kirkcolm Primary School Classes 3,4, 5, and 6, Session 1951-52. The group contains representatives of several well known local families. Kirkcolm school was established in 1872 by the Misses Moore of Corsewall House so that village and estate workers' children did not have to travel to the parish school at Mahaar. However, because it was a one-room, one-teacher school, children had to transfer to Mahaar at the age of eight or nine. This arrangement continued until 1910, when the staff was increased to two. Forty years later the school was made a junior secondary and the adjacent, former Women's Land Army Hostel acquired to provide additional classrooms. After ten years the junior secondary department closed but the primary survived unlike its parish counterparts at Mahaar and secluded Dhuloch, the latter after a 94-year existence, during which time only one register was used.

UNVEILING OF KIRKCOLM WAR MEMORIAL

Kirkcolm parish war memorial was unveiled on 26th May, 1921, on a day of perfect weather. The parish church and Free Church congregations came together for the service in the packed parish church before the actual unveiling ceremony, which was conducted by an army chaplain, Rev. Martin, seen in the centre foreground. The monument, of Creetown granite transported to Kirkcolm by local carrier W. Simpson, was unveiled by Colonel Buchanan MP of Drumpellier, a relative of the owner of Corsewall estate. On the right of the picture are the combined choirs of the two churches while invited guests on the left include the elders of both churches, the memorial committee, and Lord Stair, who had been a prisoner of war in the conflict. He may be the tall figure in the diced cap of the Scots Guards to the left of the minister.

31

COAL BOAT AT THE WIG

In a sea-girt parish like Kirkcolm sea transport was for long a vital means of communication. Small coasting vessels brought cargoes of coal and lime into Dally Bay, Lady Bay, and The Wig, beaching at high tide to unload at low water and depart on the next full tide. The Wig was particularly good for this purpose, being described in 1791 as… *a safe retreat for a great number of small craft*. The coal being unloaded here was not always the fuel used in the district for in 1837 it was recorded that the most usual type of fuel was peat. And not everyone was content with the landing arrangements for in the same year the tenants in the north-east of the parish expressed a desire, never fulfilled, for a pier at Lady Bay to facilitate the receiving and exporting of produce.

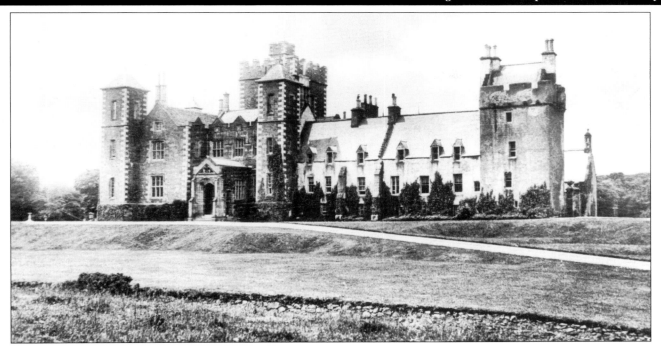

LOCHNAW CASTLE
Lochnaw Castle, the seat of the Agnew family, hereditary sheriffs of Wigtownshire for 300 years, is seen here in the 1930s at its maximum size after four major building phases. The original fifteenth century, four-storey, tower house on the right had an L-shaped extension added in 1663. The long leg of the L with its six dormer windows is clearly visible; the short leg of the L, out of sight here, ran back towards the loch. In 1704 a modest two-storey extension turned the L into a U: the top of the new leg is visible on the right of the tower house. All this was dwarfed by the huge, brick extension on the left of 1821. This last was built too late for the visit in 1746 of the Duke of Cumberland, thanking the laird for signal service pre-Culloden as defender of Blair Castle from besieging Jacobites.

33

LOCHNAW CASTLE, WEST WING
The huge size of the 1821 extension to the castle is made clear by this view of its west side. It was demolished by a post-Agnew owner around 1950 together with the 1704 extension to leave the house in its present form. Major alterations (and second thoughts) at Lochnaw were not confined to the castle. At one stage the loch itself was drained to form a meadow, only to be reinstated by a later Agnew. The surrounding gardens matched in their heyday the splendour of the expanded building, especially the Italian garden, well out of sight on the left and now a jungle of tangled vegetation. In the middle of it a commemorative stone to the garden's creator, Lady Louisa Agnew, daughter of the Earl of Gainsborough, bears with unconscious irony the Biblical quotation, "Let her own works praise her in the gates."

KINSALE TOWER

This small, circular structure stands on Craighead of Lochnaw south of the castle. It is named after Kinsale in south-west Ireland, home of Martha de Courcy, daughter of Lord Kinsale, who eloped with and married Andrew Agnew, heir to the seventh baronet of Lochnaw. Four months after the wedding her husband predeceased his father at the age of 26. The local tradition that the tower was built to allow the homesick lady to view her homeland thus seems unlikely especially since it has no interior and access to the top is by an external, hanging ladder. More probable is the tale that it was a signal station, where white sheets were displayed to inform Agnew relatives in the Larne area of the birth of a child at Lochnaw: the couple's son, who spent his early years at Kinsale, succeeded to the estate and had thirteen children.

GALDENOCH CASTLE

The small tower house, noteworthy for its crow-stepped gables and little pepper-pot turret, was built in the mid-sixteenth century by Gilbert Agnew, second son of the laird of Lochnaw and founder of the salt pans on the nearby shore. It eventually became a farmhouse on Lochnaw estate. It was the residence of the district's best known ghost, a spirit with a fondness for practical jokes. These included adding unwelcome ingredients to the contents of cooking pots and immersing one occupant's mother in the mill burn: "I've washed grannie in the burn and laid her on the dyke to dry." Repeated attempts to exorcise the unwelcome presence failed as the spirit's powerful voice drowned out the prayers and singing of the officiating clergyman. Finally a new minister at Kirkcolm, one Marshall, succeeded by virtue of possessing vocal chords of extraordinary potency.

ALDOURAN GLEN

In the heyday of the Agnews the public road through Aldouran Glen was considered by them as part of the driveway to Lochnaw Castle and the verges furnished with bulbs and plants and tended by the estate gardeners. The adjoining glen was planted with choice trees and shrubs so that it became one of the attractions of the district. On the opposite side of the glen from the road, on a promontory, is situated an Iron Age fort known as Kempes Graves. It seems likely that the original fort has been extended and re-used at a later date. Sir Andrew Agnew may therefore not have been wide of the mark in his *Hereditary Sheriffs* when he suggested that the Germanic origin of the word "Kempes" indicates Norse occupation of the site in the tenth century.

37

AGNEW MONUMENT

Situated on the Tor of Craigoch north of Leswalt, the Agnew Monument is the most prominent landmark of the North Rhinns and visible from well outside that district. It commemorates the seventh baronet, Sir Andrew, who died in 1849. As an MP from 1830 to 1837 Sir Andrew became a national and controversial figure for his vigorous promotion of the cause of Sabbath observance: the text inscribed on a panel on the monument, "Remember the Sabbath to keep it holy", is supremely appropriate. Here in Scotland he fought hard to prevent trains running on a Sunday. But he also made a major impact locally by his efforts to improve the castle, policies, and whole estate after many years of neglect. His monument stands on the site of a hill fort built 1800 years earlier.

LESWALT FROM KIRKLAND HILL
The 1930s description "the scattered houses which form the little village" is justified by this view of Leswalt before local authority and, later, private housing unified the dispersed settlement, which covered a considerable area along three routes from the crossroads. At the latter, the school and schoolhouse in the centre of the picture and the church hidden in the trees form the modern centre of the community; the house in front of the trees has been demolished. The main axis of the village stretched along the road towards the right-hand corner, where the modern graveyard is visible. The trees behind the latter conceal the old church and school, which together formed the original centre of the clachan. Kirkland farm is in the extreme left middleground with Challoch farm over on the right. The mini-complex of two houses in the centre foreground formerly included a shop.

39

LESWALT FREE CHURCH ·

At the Disruption of 1843, when the Free Church was created, Leswalt was in an unusual position for the local landed proprietor, "the gude Sir Andra" Agnew, favoured the new establishment and not only provided land for a church but built one together with a manse. It was of a standard type with three parallel ranges and no internal walls, the roofs supported on cast iron pillars. The small building in the foreground is the church hall, where at one time the Literary and Debating Society met. On the opposite side of the road Sir Andrew built a stable to accommodate churchgoers' horses; the gigs stood at the roadside. In the church grounds the presence of a monument to Sir Andrew's wife, Lady Madeline, suggests she may have made a major financial contribution to the building. An early minister, Alexander Warrack, compiled a Scots dictionary still in print.

LESWALT, WEST END

The west end of Leswalt is the former centre of the village with the old church (almost invisible in the trees behind the wall on the left) and old school (of which only a dormer window can be seen between the first and second houses). The first house is now demolished. The second carries the date 1861, by which time the village centre of gravity was moving east towards the crossroads. On the right of the large trees, the one-storey building, a former stables block, became the carpet bowling hall and then in World War Two was the venue for prayer meetings for service personnel held by local evangelist William Scott, where he weekly enacted the local version of the loaves and fishes miracle by feeding the multitude with sandwiches and pancakes. Aldouran House, the estate dower residence, can be glimpsed in the trees behind.

LESWALT OLD PARISH CHURCH

This south-east corner of Leswalt old parish church, with a burial vault to the east, is much less photogenic than the northern view of the building, dominated by the Agnew aisle, which can offer in its gable an elegant window and a panel bearing the date 1644 with the names of Patrick Agnew and his spouse Margaret Kennedy. The first floor of the aisle comprised the lairds' loft while underneath was the family burial vault. The church itself, probably of sixteenth century date, stands on the site of an older building for documentary evidence reveals that Leswalt church was annexed to Tongland Abbey in the 1350s. The panel reference to a presumably amicable union between an Agnew and a Kennedy is ironical for a bitter and protracted dispute festered between the two families over the right to hold courts here in Leswalt.

LESWALT SCHOOL

Today's Leswalt school differs from this version in the disappearance of the chimney stack in the centre and demise of the small hut on the right, which served as cook house and dining hall and also as classroom for practical subjects. Leswalt did not have a proper school building until 1776, when one was built immediately east of the old church. It still stands today, much altered and now a private house. For a time after the closure of the old church in 1828, the latter was used to house the school, perhaps while its usual home was undergoing alteration. In the 1790s the building was not required full-time for it is recorded that the children attended school for five months and for the rest of the year were kept off to assist their parents in "country matters". The present school was built in 1872-5.

43

LESWALT SCHOOL GROUP

Pupils from "The Wee End" of Leswalt school in session 1923-24 parade for the camera while headmaster HS Hall eyes the photographer warily. Class teacher Miss McHarg is on the left. The first-ever Leswalt parish school teacher in 1724 was Matthew Cunningham. Eight years later his successor Robert Hunter was able to teach Latin, giving Leswalt the advantages of a grammar school. One of the institution's more unusual alumni was David Kennedy, born 1817, son of the engineer in charge of building Corsewall lighthouse. He joined from Kirkcolm school at the age of eleven and at seventeen emigrated with his family to Canada. From Canada he moved across the frontier to Philadelphia, where he found his vocation as a painter of portraits and landscapes. One of his earliest paintings of "Leswalt Academy, Gallowayshire, Scotland" now reposes in the Boston Museum of Fine Arts.

LESWALT POST OFFICE

Although Leswalt parish had no post office at the end of the eighteenth century, the deficiency was eventually remedied. Here it is sited in one of the group of five houses situated between Challoch farm and the church. It was presided over in the 1930s and 1940s by Mrs Biggam and then Mrs Agnew before its location was shifted to Isles Cottage close to Kirkland farm on the Ervie road. Its next move was to its present location. The sign "Leswalt Post Office", offset above the door, was 'til recently displayed on a nearby outbuilding. The other sign announces that the office has telegraph facilities (something no modern equivalent can offer) while the left-hand window suggests that the building also operated as a shop. An impressive display of environmentally friendly transport complements the scene.

45

LESWALT PASTORAL

The dispersed nature of the pre-war village made a picture of Leswalt something of a challenge but the photographer here has hardly risen to it: the centre of the photograph is occupied by an equally dispersed herd of horned, Ayrshire cattle, a modern rarity. The cluster of buildings in the centre background is unarguably Kirkland farm steading with the dairyhouse on the right although the former farmhouse itself is strangely absent, possibly hidden in the trees. The angle suggests the picture was taken from the spot where the Memorial Hall, opened in 1927, now stands. The house on the right is still identifiable while that on the left has been transformed into the village shop. Just to the left of the right-hand house the former Free Church manse, Kirkland House, perhaps announces its presence at the edge of the tall trees.

46